REALITY AND ILLUSION

DIVYANSH SINGH

Made with ❤ on the Notion Press Platform
www.notionpress.com

Dedicated to Worthy

Children of Mother Earth

And my Mother *Mrs. Krishna Singh's* Legacy.

Contents

Preface

What is this book?

This book tries to make you understand The Realities And Illusions of the Almighty Nature. And Tries to explain about the illusions that we have, which are, We are the ones who do work, We have established justice, We are independent in doing anything, We are not controlled, We are free, etc. If I say that all we do is already programmed and there is nothing that we do. And If I may say that you are in an Illusion if you think that you are free. And in this book, I will try to convince you by giving logical arguments for the same.

In this world of Uniqueness, if there are billions of people out there on Planet, then it is most probable that each individual has their own sets of thoughts, which means a billion ways to think. Now, if you try to name all those kinds of thinking, you will have to invent billions of words to describe them. And that is a tedious task to do. So, you are bound to have different perspectives. Thus, it is also most probable that you may not get convinced, and I am fine with that. As an element of this ecosystem, I try to find a unique pattern of differences among those billions, through this book, which can connect them all.

CHAPTER ONE

BEING CONTROLLED

All the creatures of Nature have a nature, The nature of being controlled. All of us are driven by our five senses and permutations and combinations of them. In every aspect of Life, In every kind of life, from small insects to a large elephants, from microorganisms to complex human beings. As the complexity of the body increases, more controllers get to work.

Every creature from Dawn to Dusk follows the cycle of senses. From waking up to going to sleep, it is our emotions, the result of our senses, driving us. In every creature the first emotion is fear, the fear to lose the body that it has. That fear of getting killed is the strongest one. We notice it or not every instance of time, we care for our security.

Whatever we do is the result of all the emotions, senses, and experiences developed in every creature from birth. In order to eat, sleep, and different life processes, designed in a way to keep you alive, we automatically are programmed to do the tasks that we do in our whole life.

So, we can all agree that we do nothing. Everything that we do is already programmed within. The programmer here is Nature, but if you can become Nature then you can reprogram it, obviously. We will talk about this in the coming chapters before that.

So, cannot we get out of this cycle? Yes, we can, by controlling all our senses. Suppose you are too hungry, have not eaten for 3 days, and you get food, can you stop yourself from eating? Suppose you have not slept for 3 days, and finally, you get a comfortable place to sleep, can you stop yourself from sleeping? So, the most probable answer will be No, as a body needs that.

But you need to develop a stronger emotion, that is above all, then you may be able to control all the senses.

So, the Reality of Life is just living it in a way that is being controlled. Realizing it is the first step to controlling the senses. But wait, there is also one thing, you will ask what you will get when you get control of your senses. Because, unless we get something, we do not do anything, that is also an emotion, you need to counter yourself.

CHAPTER TWO

ROOT OF ALL PROBLEMS

In all Ecosystems, may that be of any class of organisms. There are issues, which result in a form of different chaos. If we look at the root causes of all the problems in every kind of ecosystem, we will notice a pattern, a unique one, that applies to all. And that root cause is the virtue of the physical body, or you can say the root cause is their physical body or the thought of being the physical body.

Or, in more depth, you can say the 'Identity', who they are is the root cause. Let me explain to you by taking Human Ecosystem as an example. You can guess any problem in Human Society and now look. If all Humans accept that they are not physical bodies, instead they are part of the universe, then now look will there be any problem?

Like - if we only look at every human as also part of the universe and think of ourselves as not a physical body, but instead something beyond it. Then, there will not be any discrimination, Racism, Gender inequality, etc.

You can examine all the problems of society and then you will find that the root cause is the same. Also, you may assume any problem of any organism, you may conclude it, and find the root cause, then it should be the same.

CHAPTER THREE

THE CONCEPT OF JUSTICE

From the beginning of life, there is always a demand for justice. In Human society, there are various arrangements for justice. But let's not limit justice to only humans, Let's expand it to other organisms as well. Well, That process is complicated, but note I am not saying it is impossible to do.

Different people will have different definitions of justice. And Even different countries in human society have different arrangements for justice.

But let's talk about justice in all ecosystems of Nature. Before that let me ask you a question. Suppose you fed some food to a bird, and that bird came down to eat the food. And then suddenly a cat starts running towards that bird to eat her. Now, you are standing there and watching, what will you do in that situation in order to give justice?

Will you save the bird from the cat? If yes then what about the food for the cat, will you give food to the cat as well? If yes then suppose at the same time a dog rushes towards the cat to eat her. Will you save the cat also? If yes then you should give food to the dog as well.

Now think about how you will do justice to animals who are hunted by carnivores like lions. You cannot feed Vegetarian food to lions.

At one point we all agree that justice should be given to all the creatures of nature. But what we see in the food cycle of Nature, is complete injustice for one in order for justice for another. So, Nature balances both justice and injustice, so is it justice?

So, Now I ask, is there justice in the world or injustice, what will be your answer? - think about that.

CHAPTER FOUR

REALITY OR ILLUSION

An organism born in an ecosystem. It may be in Animal Ecosystem, Bird Ecosystem, Human Ecosystem, or any other Species Ecosystem. All of the Ecosystems have a structure that is needed to keep them intact and make them unique.

All of the species will do their work that is already decided by Nature, but still, there is a uniqueness of emotions that all will have. Now, if an element of an ecosystem tries to break the rules or structure of that ecosystem, the rest of the elements are going to neutralize it.

Among all the species Human beings are the ones with the most complicated ecosystem, thus the most complicated structure. In this Ecosystem as well, all will have to follow the rules and structure built by Nature. They will behave as Nature wants them to behave.

As they are bound by some virtues of Nature. Again if an element of this ecosystem defies the already built structure, the rest will neutralize it, And if the whole ecosystem of human beings tries to defy(that is very rare) Nature, then

Nature will have to neutralize that ecosystem herself.

Now, here is an interesting scenario, let's suppose an element of some ecosystem tries to defy the structure of that ecosystem and as well is not following Nature's laws. Now when I say not following Nature's laws I mean, an element of some ecosystem, by some means got successful in getting out of the range of Nature's virtues.

That means he is now independent of the influence of the Ecosystem as well as Nature. Now, Nature cannot neutralize it. Thus, that element is set to become Nature itself. Now, to know how that Element got out of the Range of Nature's virtues, you should look at the concept of Reality and Illusion.

Let me explain - Nature has one virtue to make all the Ecosystems, that means all the elements of it feel that it is independent of doing all work that they think it real. And makes it believe they did it, so no doubt remains.

Now, if that reality is different for each element, then all of them will start living in their own illusionistic world. Now there remains no loop-holes, so no chance of undisciplined elements. But what if an element has an illusionistic world that came out to be real. As the number of elements increases, the probability will rise. Thus, that element outplays the Nature.

CHAPTER FIVE

THE HARDEST TEST OR THE HARDEST PUNISHMENT

If an element of some ecosystem tries to defy some predefined rules, then to neutralize that element there are a set of punishments. Some punishments kill them, some torture them and more severe punishments are on the list, to neutralize those elements and set an example of them. So that no other element of that ecosystem dares to misadventure.

But what if I give you another way to punish that? Let's suppose that you are not any organism, instead, you are something that is immortal, non-materialistic, and never-born. Then, suppose you need to be punished.

And Now here I apply my punishment. You are placed in such a container that is materialistic. If anything happens to the container, it will feel you. And I give you emotions, that is you do not want to get out of the container.

Now, previously when you were non-materialistic you did not feel anything so you were safer. Now, things have changed. Now, I am going to add more such elements whom I am punishing in connection with you.

I also give them containers like you and make all these elements in connection such that all of you will have to feel each other's problem and react to it. Now, I also add the reaction of each action you do via your container.

And those reactions are going to directly affect your container, thus giving rise to different kinds of emotions that will work to keep you intact with the container and with the cycle of those emotions.

Till now you will have understood what container I am talking about, it is none other than an organism's life in different kinds of ecosystems.

Now, Let's talk about another perspective, that is, suppose you are a student of some element of an ecosystem. And you are being taught and trained to carry out certain kinds of operations.

Now your master trained you and then wants to evaluate your skills to confirm if you can carry out certain operations or not.

Now as the operation is big, the master is going to test everything, from bottom to up, across each and every particle in you. Now there are different kinds of tests to test someone.

Now, here I give you a new method to test some elements, that will guarantee your success in that mission. That I put that element into the same container, which I was using for punishment. And whoever is able to come out of that container and control each and every action and thus reaction, passes the test.

Now, Tell me, are you giving a test or are you going through your punishment? Tell me if you want to get success in your test or you want to bear it thinking as punishment.